DINGHY SAILING
FOR
BEGINNERS

DINGHY SAILING
FOR
BEGINNERS

CAMPBELL L. WAIDE

A GENERAL INTRODUCTION
TO DINGHY SAILING
FOR PEOPLE OF ALL AGES

WITH ILLUSTRATIONS BY THE AUTHOR

ARTHUR H. STOCKWELL Ltd.,
Elms Court   Ilfracombe,
Devon

ISBN 0 7223 0861-2
Printed in Great Britain by
Arthur H. Stockwell Ltd
Elms Court   Ilfracombe
Devon

ACKNOWLEDGEMENTS

My thanks are due to *IPC Newspapers Ltd.* of London, for permission to use details of their Mirror Class dinghy, and to the Plymouth Meteorological Office for the Table of Percentage Frequency of Winds and information on weather forecasts; to Gina Kingdon for deciphering my scribble and doing such a neat typing job; to Karen Wheeler for assisting with the illustrations; to Her Majesty's Stationery Office, London, for permission to use extracts from the International Code of Signals, 1969 Edition.

FOREWORD

In this cleverly illustrated book Campbell L. Waide, who is 69 years young, a retired Civil Servant and still sailing a very fast sailing dinghy, a National Scorpion, is sharing the pleasure of his experience, which is in itself a pleasure. That is why I am sure the author, who has spent many hours and days putting into this book in words and pictures all the enjoyment he has had in forty years of sailing, would feel very satisfied if, through its words and pictures, he had encouraged anyone, especially the young, to go sailing.

Sailing is the supreme sport and the youngsters of today in small boats are the Chichesters and Blyths of tomorrow.

JAMES L. EDGAR
Commodore
Royal Plymouth Corinthian Yacht Club,
Plymouth.
April, 1974

CONTENTS

LIST OF ILLUSTRATIONS

INTRODUCTION

In the preparation of this book the author had in mind the need for some simple explanations, not too verbose and avoiding technicalities which only bore the reader, with easily understood diagrams for the newcomer to the sport of dinghy sailing and, in particular, the needs of the beginner from whom will develop the yachtsmen and yachtswomen of the future. It is felt that beginners should be given every opportunity and encouragement to get afloat and enjoy the sport.

To those parents, or fond grandparents, who may be racking their brains as to what to give for a special birthday present, have you considered giving 'sailing lessons' at a school of sailing next time you go on summer holidays to the seaside? Most seaside towns have very good sailing schools that provide boats, competent instructors and all the gear required, at a very reasonable fee.

To the newcomer to the sport, it should be mentioned that you are entering a world where a new language is used (I mean new to you, of course) i.e., the language of the sea with all its nautical terms, where a simple rope is no longer a rope but a 'sheet' or a 'halyard' and looking from the stern, the blunt end, the left side of the boat is 'port' and the right side is 'starboard'! Go to it and enjoy it, have fun, and good sailing.

Chapter 1

THE BOAT

The type of boat chosen in this book for the purpose of illustrating the art of dinghy sailing is the very popular Mirror Class dinghy.

This craft is built of marine plywood and has a length of 10ft 10in. and a width (beam) of 4ft 7in. It has a mainsail of 49 sq.ft. and is easily handled by quite young helmsmen. The hull weighs only 98 lbs. and the complete boat weighs 135 lbs. There are over 51,000 Mirror Class dinghies in use all over the world and that, obviously, proves their popularity.

See figure 1. This drawing gives the various parts of the boat. You should memorize them for they will be referred to from time to time.

This boat was designed by a team consisting of Barry Bucknell, Bernard Hayman (Editor of Yachting World), and Jack Holt, one of the world's foremost yacht designers. Proof of this dinghy's buoyancy was demonstrated recently when twenty-one members of a certain sailing club, all wearing life-jackets, crowded into one, and it still remained afloat. (Page 5 of the Yachting and Boating weekly magazine of 16 January 1974.)

The Mirror dinghy was chosen because it is considered to be the ideal type of craft for the beginner because of its low initial cost and its ease of handling both in and out of the water due to its light weight and manoeuvrability.

Chapter 2

THE WIND AND THE SAILS
*Means of propulsion, Beaufort wind scale,
local Wind Rose*

It is assumed that when you take the boat out for your first attempt at sailing you will have someone with you who has had some experience of dinghy sailing, otherwise you could soon be in trouble, which should be avoided. So be wise and arrange for someone to go with you to take the tiller and instruct you to begin with, and you act as crew.

Now is the time when you will come face to face with one of the elements — the wind — which will play a great part in your life in the future as you continue to sail. Up to now, no doubt, you have taken the wind for granted; now you have to give it a lot of consideration, and to think about it. Is it a good sailing wind? From which direction is it coming? You must instantly be able to locate the line of the wind in order to sail efficiently. You can tell by observing such tell-tale things as flags flying on near-by flag poles or smoke from chimneys and the movements of other sailing craft.

You could try a simple test by turning to face the wind and then slowly turning your head from side to side to get the feel of the wind. After a little experience you will find that you can point straight up-wind, i.e., the direction from which the wind is blowing at you.

This is a good point at which to impress on you the important fact that everything to do with sailing is related to the wind. Wind is the means of propulsion and it can help you, or hinder you. It all depends on how you use it. Only by practice and experience will you learn to use it correctly and efficiently.

It might help you to make up your mind as to whether it is a good sailing wind by studying the Beaufort wind scale. You will see from the various wind forces that there are times when it is not safe to sail.

BEAUFORT WIND SCALE

Beaufort force	Wind description	Wind speed	
		knots	mph
0	Calm	0	0
1	Light airs	1-3	1-3
2	Light Breeze	4-6	4-7
3	Gentle Breeze	7-10	8-12
4	Moderate breeze	11-16	13-18
5	A fresh breeze	17-21	19-24
6	A strong breeze	22-27	25-31
7	Near gale	28-33	32-38
8	Gale	34-40	39-46
9	Severe gale	41-47	47-54
10	Storm	48-56	55-63
11	Violent storm	57-65	64-75
12	Hurricane	OVER 65	OVER 75

Note:
The Beaufort scale of wind velocity ranging from 0 (calm) to 12 (hurricane — 75 miles an hour or over) was prepared by Sir F. Beaufort, an English Admiral, who died in 1857.

If you listen to the weather forecast for shipping you will hear the wind force mentioned, and when checked against the table above, you will be able to decide if the wind is suitable for sailing your type of dinghy. If the wind is above force 4 you would be wise, as a beginner, to stay at home.

Now we come to the other factor involved in the propulsion of the boat — the sails.

In figure 2 the sails are shown and they consist of "A" the mainsail and "B" the jib. This is a simple layout that is easily handled. Study the details and remember the names of the various parts of the sails.

In the old days sails were made of canvas which, when wet, became heavy and stiff and hard to handle; it also tended to go mouldy and rot. Nowadays most modern dinghy sails are made of Terylene which does not absorb water and is much easier and lighter to handle.

WIND ROSE, THE PREVAILING WIND

As you know, the wind blows from different directions throughout the year and from one direction for longer periods than from other directions. This is known as the prevailing wind.

The wind directions over the year can be charted from the records kept by the Meteorological Offices. (See Chart on page 21.) The information in this chart was used to prepare the Wind Rose for Plymouth for the years 1965-69, figure 4. This is based on a compass circle and shows wind directions and wind speeds over a period of time during which the wind forces operated from the various directions, north, south, east, west.

From the Wind Rose it will be seen that the winds blow from all points of the compass during the year, but mainly from south-south-west, then south-west and west, from which direction the percentage frequency is as much as 35.1 per cent and covering a speed range from 0 to force 9.

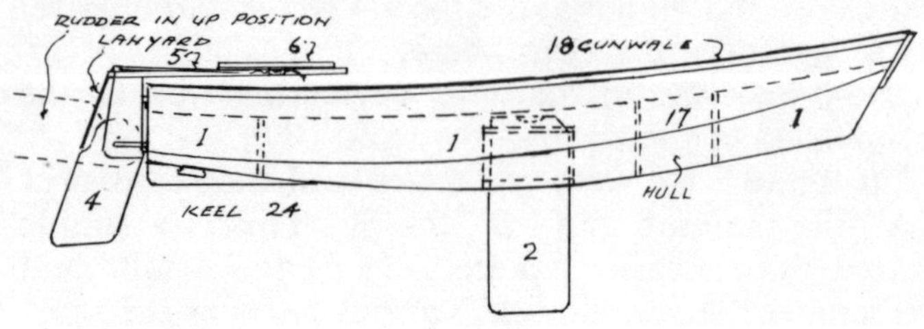

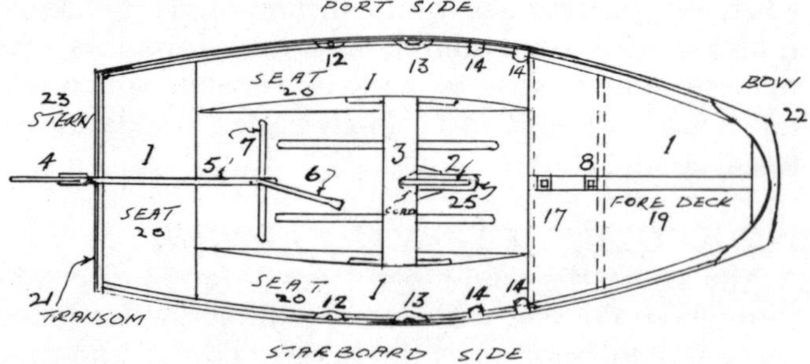

FIGURE 1
PARTS OF THE BOAT

1. Buoyancy tanks
2. Centre-board
3. Thwart (used as seat)
4. Retractable rudder
5. Tiller
6. Tiller extension
7. Footrest
8. Forward mast stop
9. Mast (see Fig. 2)
10. Boom (see Fig. 2)
11. Gaff (see Fig. 2)
12. Rowlocks (when using oars)
13. Fairleads (for jib sheets)
14. Shroud plates
15. Sail Battens (see Fig. 2)
16. Gooseneck
17. Dry storage
18. Gunwale
19. Fore deck
20. Seats
21. Transom
22. Bow
23. Stern
24. Keel
25. Centre-board casing

RACING FLAG
RACING FLAG
CLUB BURGEE IN VARIOUS DESIGNS
PARTS OF THE SAILS
HEAD
4
6"
18"
GAFF
11
TRACK
15
HEAD
SAIL BATTEN
FORESTAY
15
LUFF HANKS
LEECH
"A" MAINSAIL
LUFF
9 MAST
LUFF
15
LEECH OF JIB
"B" JIB FORESAIL
SHROUD
CLEW
10 BOOM
TACK
16 GOOSENECK
FOOT
TACK
MAINSHEET
JIB SHEET
CLEW OF JIB
FOOT
KICKING STRAP
W.L.
W.L.

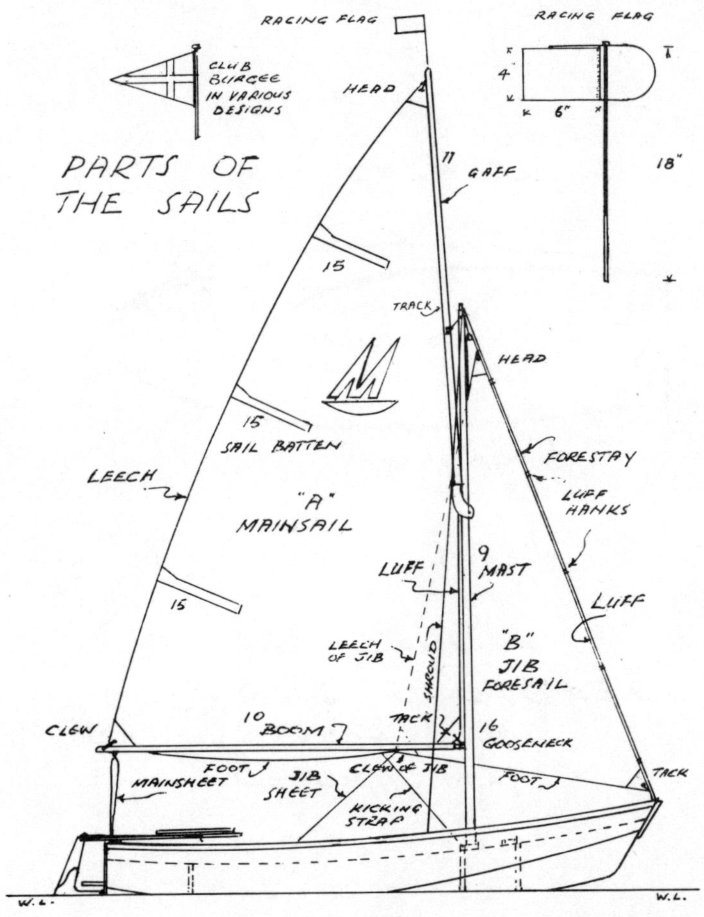

FIGURE 2

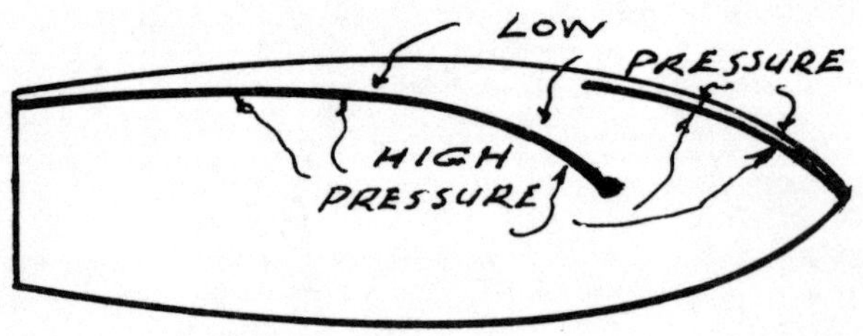

FIGURE 3
AEROFOIL SHAPE
OF SAILS
CLOSE HAULED

PERCENTAGE FREQUENCY OF WINDS AT MOUNT BATTEN, PLYMOUTH 1965 - 1969
(5 years) — ALL HOURS — WHOLE YEAR

Winds are hourly mean winds recorded by the electrical anemograph at Fort Stamford (NGR SX 492527) Height of Cups: Above Ground 42 feet: Above MSL 209 feet. Effective Height 42 feet.

Mean Wind Speed

Percentage number of hours with winds from

knots	mph	Bft force	350°-010°	020°-040°	050°-070°	080°-100°	110°-130°	140°-160°	170°-190°	200°-220°	230°-250°	260°-280°	290°-310°	320°-340°	All directions
	Calm														7.9
1-3	1-3	1	0.5	0.5	0.6	0.9	0.3	0.1	0.1	0.4	0.4	0.6	0.6	0.7	5.5
4-6	4-7	2	1.3	1.0	1.3	2.3	0.8	0.4	0.3	1.4	1.1	1.4	1.3	1.6	14.4
7-10	8-12	3	2.1	1.4	1.7	3.0	1.7	1.2	1.1	3.4	2.5	2.8	1.9	2.3	25.1
11-16	13-18	4	1.5	0.9	1.8	3.3	1.8	1.8	1.9	3.4	4.7	3.7	2.8	2.5	30.1
17-21	19-24	5	0.3	0.1	0.4	0.9	0.4	0.3	1.0	1.4	1.9	1.5	1.0	0.7	10.0
22-27	25-31	6	0.1	<.1	0.1	0.4	0.1	0.1	0.4	0.9	1.4	0.8	0.6	0.3	5.2
28-33	32-38	7	<.1	<.1		0.1	<.1	<.1	0.1	0.3	0.5	0.2	0.1	<.1	1.4
34-40	39-46	8	<.1				<.1	<.1	0.1	0.1	0.1	<.1			0.3
41-47	47-54	9							<.1	<.1	<.1	<.1			<.1
48-55	55-63	10													0.0
56-63	64-72	11													0.0
>63	>72	>11													0.0
Totals, all speeds			5.7	4.0	5.9	10.8	5.0	4.0	5.1	11.4	12.6	11.1	8.4	8.1	100.0

PERCENTAGE FREQUENCY OF WINDS
FOR PLYMOUTH 1965-1969 (5 YEARS)
ALL HOURS WHOLE YEAR ALL DIRECTIONS ALL SPEEDS

WIND ROSE

DEVELOPED FROM INFORMATION SUPPLIED
BY THE METEOROLOGICAL OFFICE PLYMOUTH

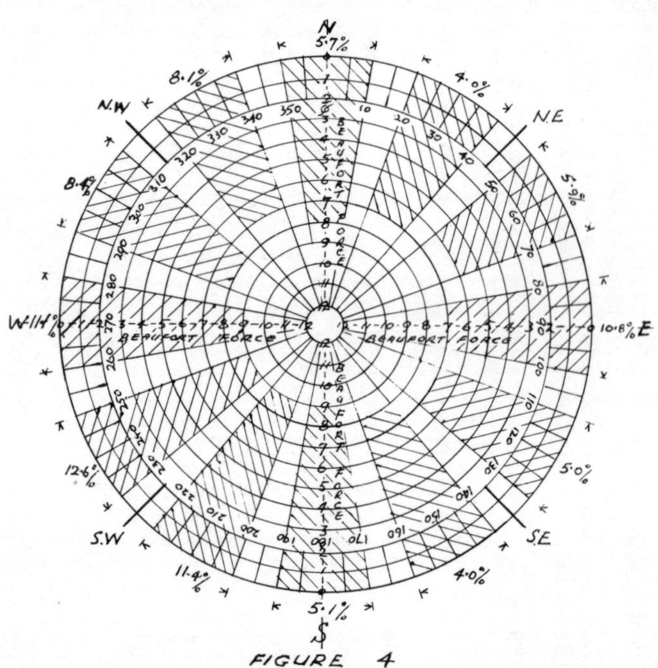

FIGURE 4

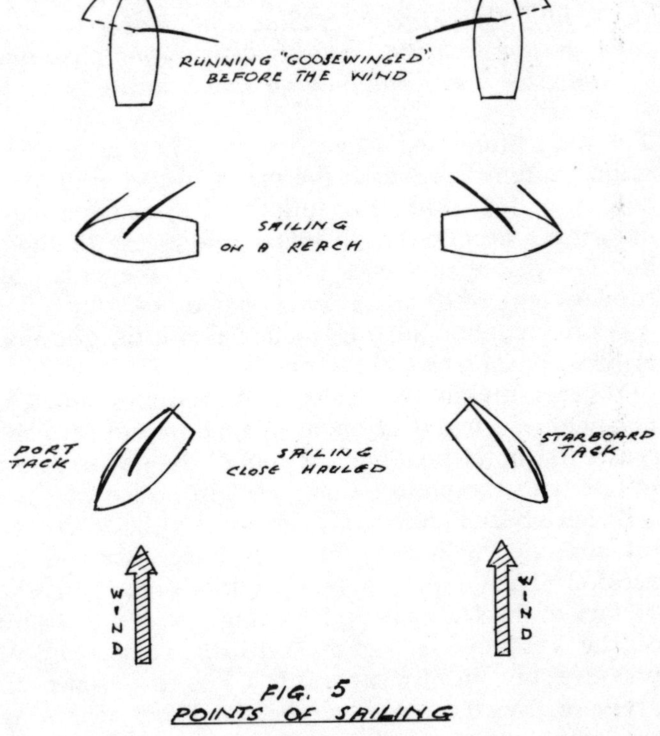

FIG. 5
POINTS OF SAILING

Chapter 3

USING THE WIND

Points of sailing, wind direction, tacking, reaching, running, gybing, in irons, broaching, lee and weather shore, luff, luffing up and spilling wind, helmsman and crew responsibilities, weight distribution, coming alongside a jetty and picking up a mooring buoy

The main thing you have to avoid when in a small sailing dinghy is being at the mercy of the wind! The only way to avoid this unfortunate and perhaps dangerous situation, is to know how to use the boat and everything that goes with it, i.e., the sails, the rudder, centre-board, the oars or paddles.

A brief mention must be made here on the question of how the sails propel the boat.

When a dinghy, or yacht, is sailing close-hauled, i.e., with the mainsail boom trimmed close into the centre line of the boat and the foot of the jib hardened in line with the main boom, you will notice that the sails have become curved, from front to back, by the pressure of the wind. The sails have assumed an aerofoil shape and the flow of the wind over the surface of the sails sets up a local increase in pressure on the windward side of the sails and a decrease of pressure on the leeward side. The difference in pressure gives the 'lift' which has the effect of moving the boat forward. See figure 3.

In simple terms, one can compare the sail of a boat with the wing of an aeroplane. It is well known that the wing of a plane gives it 'lift' to rise off the ground and stay in the air, whereas the sails of a boat close-hauled give it 'lift', but the 'lift' acts sideways in a dinghy and is resisted by the centre-board which has been lowered into the water below the hull. The result is that the boat moves forward.

The first step towards achieving the 'know how' regarding the use of the boat and the sails et cetera is to learn the basic points of sailing, which are:

(a) Sailing close-hauled

(b) Reaching

(c) Running before the wind.

These three points are best illustrated by the drawings in figure 5, but before going any further into these basic points of sailing it will be useful to deal with the question of wind direction in relation to the hull of the boat.

In yachting terms the wind is said to be, if heading into the wind, 'to windward', 'abeam', or on port or starboard bow, and with wind astern boat heads to 'leeward', or on port or starboard quarter. Experienced sailors usually refer to leeward as 'loo'ard'.

The illustration in figure 7 depicts this in a clear and simple manner.

(a) *SAILING CLOSE-HAULED*

In figure 7 you will see that the boat is pointing directly into the wind. Now to begin with you must realize that a boat cannot sail directly into the wind. So what must you do to make progress? It has been found that sailing boats will usually sail at an angle of about 45 degrees to the wind direction.

To explain this turn to figure 9. The object is to sail from buoy A to buoy B. The wind is dead ahead, so in order to make way the boat has to be turned at an angle of 45 degrees to the line of the wind, and with the sails trimmed hard in you are sailing 'close-hauled' and 'beating to windward'. Your course is in the form of a zigzag, and you tack from port to starboard as you progress. The centre-board must be lowered right down when sailing close-hauled to resist side thrust and reduce leeway.

It should be mentioned here that the centre-board is provided to act as a keel, the purpose being to resist side thrust on the sails by the pressure of the wind, but it should be understood that even with a keel, or centre-board, in a dinghy there will always be a certain degree of sideways 'slip' away from the wind to leeward and hence it is called 'leeway'.

This means that when you are sailing close-hauled, or on a reach, you must make allowance for leeway when making for any particular mark or destination. You do this by steering to windward of the mark to such a degree that you judge will bring you to the mark.

The term 'port and starboard tack' means that when the wind is blowing on the mainsail on the port side and the mainsail boom is angled over to the starboard side of the boat, you are said to be on the 'port tack', and with the wind on the starboard side and the boom angled to the port side, you are on the 'starboard tack'.

Now let us get back to figure 9 and take this action step by step. You are approaching buoy A close-hauled on a starboard tack (position 1), having cleared the buoy you bring the boat 'head to wind' (position 2). This is called 'luffing up'. This is part of the manoeuvre known as 'going about' and changing from port tack to starboard tack and vice versa. You have turned the boat through 45 degrees. You now have to complete the action by turning the boat's bow through the eye of the wind to get on to 'port tack' to complete the 90 degrees turn and sail away close-hauled on port tack (position 3). You repeat this manoeuvre through positions 4, 5, 6 and 7 to complete the run from buoy A to buoy B.

This seems to be a good point at which to mention the method of handling the jib sheets and mainsail sheet. The crew handling the jib sheets may fix them in the jamming cleat but the helmsman in a dinghy should *never* fix the main sheet — this must always be held by him. If the main sheet was fixed it could be dangerous and lead to a capsize if quick action was needed to spill wind or go about in an emergency.

(b) *REACHING*

The term 'reaching' is generally applied to the condition when the wind is on the beam (see figure 6). To get the best results you should angle out the mainsail boom at about 35 degrees (see figure 5) and trim the jib out so that the foot is in the same line as the foot of the mainsail.

With the wind on the beam, as in this case, it is usually referred to as a 'beam reach', which is one of the fastest points of sailing. Under these conditions the centre-board should be raised about half-way up, to reduce the drag. There are two other aspects of reaching:

(1) *Close reaching* when the wind is on the port, or starboard, bow but not fine enough to be close-hauled (see figure 6). Raise the centre-board about a quarter up.

(2) *Broad reaching* when the wind is on the port, or starboard, quarter (figure 6). The sails should

be angled out even further than in the beam reach. Centre-board up about three-quarters.

(c) *RUNNING BEFORE THE WIND*

The third point of sailing is when the wind is astern, i.e., blowing from the stern area, and the boat is sailing 'before the wind'. Under these conditions the mainsail boom should be angled out until it is almost at right angles to the boat (see figure 5). In this case the centre-board should be raised right up as there is no sideways thrust from the wind.

On this point of sailing the mainsail blankets off the jib and so a different technique is required in trimming the jib. This requires a light-weight pole about 5ft long, referred to as a 'whisker pole' or 'jib stick'. The clew of the jib is fixed to one end of the stick and the other end of the stick is fixed to the mast, near the gooseneck of the boom; the jib is then trimmed out on the opposite side to the mainsail and you are then sailing running 'goosewinged' (figure 5).

To help clarify the above points, it would be useful to combine all the four positions for trimming the sails into one illustration as shown in figure 6. This gives easy comparison for sailing on a selected course with various wind directions in relation to the selected course.

Having explained the various main points of sailing, we now have to consider some other aspects of sailing which, without doubt, you will meet very early in your sailing days. The first is the 'gybe' and then getting 'in irons' and 'broaching'.

GYBING

With the wind astern, or on the quarter, a gybe is performed when you change the course upon which you are sailing by swinging the stern of the boat through the eye of the wind, thus causing the boom to swing from one side to the other. This manoeuvre can be done deliberately and uncontrolled or controlled, but very often it is done accidentally when the boom swings across from one side to the other with a bang! An accidental gybe often results in a capsize, especially in a strong wind, so great care must be taken when running before the wind.

It should be understood that gybing is a recognized manoeuvre in sailing and you must by now appreciate the difference between tacking and gybing. In tacking the boat's *bow* swings up through the eye of the wind and in gybing it is the *stern* of the boat which is swung through the eye of the wind. In both actions you change the tack upon which you were sailing.

It would be helpful to enlarge on the three aspects of gybing, i.e., the accidental gybe, the deliberate and the uncontrolled gybe, and the controlled gybe. The accidental gybe occurs when, by the carelessness of the helmsman in a run before the wind, the wind is allowed to back the mainsail and the boom slams across to the other side. This could result in a capsize or a broken mast.

In a deliberate but uncontrolled gybe the helmsman takes action to make a quick turn in a race, or in an emergency such as when someone falls overboard and a speedy recovery is vital.

In a controlled gybe the helmsman takes action to hand the boom across at the same time sheeting in the main sheet to reduce the swing of the boom and so reduce the arc of the swing and thus avoid the violence of the 'slam' that would otherwise occur. So be warned, avoid accidental gybes and don't attempt an uncontrolled gybe until you have had considerable experience of sailing in all conditions. See figure 8 which illustrates a controlled gybe around a mark buoy.

IN IRONS

This condition usually occurs when 'going about' or tacking and when beating to windward when the boat is head to wind and the helmsman has misjudged the move and the 'way' has been taken off the boat. You have stopped, the rudder has become useless and you are out of control. You are said to be 'in irons'. However, this condition will not last long, for very soon the wind will start pushing the boat backwards. Whatever you do don't panic because as soon as the boat starts moving backwards it becomes possible to steer backwards and you have control again. With the correct use of the tiller she can be made to 'pay off' on one tack or the other according to the conditions, space to manoeuvre et cetera existing at the time. Also the boat will inevitably swing across the wind and you can start sailing again. It would help to 'back the jib' to get moving again.

BROACHING, BROACH TO

The dictionary defines 'broaching to' as causing a ship, or boat, to veer and present the side to the wind and waves. This can happen accidentally in a sailing dinghy, and again could cause a capsize. It usually happens when gybing, for immediately after the gybe the tendency is for the boat to turn into the wind, which you must counter by quick action on the helm to keep the bows pointing down wind.

LEE AND WEATHER SHORE

Figure 10 shows two shores which might be the opposite sides of a non-tidal lake, with the wind direction at right angles to the shores. When the wind is *blowing off the land* that is referred to as the 'weather shore' and when the wind is blowing *on to the land* it is referred to as the 'lee shore'.

For the dinghy sailor problems arise when the water is shallow near the beach on a 'lee' or a 'weather shore'.

Let us take the case of the weather shore first (boat A in figure 10). If you want to sail *away* from the shore it is easy because the wind will blow you off the shore. You can start by 'backing the jib' and you head away from shore. As you are in shallow water the centre-board will be right up, ease off the main sheet and sail off down wind until you reach deep water and then lower the centre-board to sail close-hauled, or on a reach according to your destination.

Sailing *on to* a weather shore, (boat B) requires quite different tactics. It is assumed that you are sailing parallel to the shore (position 1) and you wish to land. Having selected your landing place you steer the boat head to wind (position 2) and as you get into shallow water the centre-board must be raised right up. The momentum will carry the boat on to the beach or your crew can step out, to stop the boat grounding when the water is shallow enough to permit this action. Do not forget to raise the rudder part-way when in shallow water, enough to keep it clear of the beach.

In the case of the *lee shore* the technique of landing and sailing off is somewhat different again. We should study figure 10 and first deal with boat C sailing towards the lee shore on a reach, going fast in a good wind, from position 1. You must 'bring up' the boat head to wind, lower the mainsail, position 2, and turn her to run ashore under the jib, position 3, raising the centre-board as you get into shallow water.

In the case of boat D sailing *off the lee shore* the correct tack is to sail off close-hauled to port or starboard, according to your destination, with the crew lowering the centre-board gradually as you get into deeper water and the helmsman doing the same with the rudder. But before you are able to sail off under these conditions, i.e., in shallow water and the wind at right angles to the shore line, it is usually found necessary to push the boat off into the wind, with a good hefty shove and a quick jump in over the stern to sheet in the main and get her sailing. Alternatively you could use paddles or oars to get into deep water and then sail off.

LUFF, LUFFING UP AND SPILLING WIND

To luff means to turn the helm in order to bring the boat's head nearer the eye of the wind. We have dealt with the question of 'luffing up' in connection with tacking and we now have to consider the action required when wind conditions are somewhat 'gusty' when a sudden strengthening wind force heels the boat to leeward to such a degree that it could be dangerous and cause a capsize. You are required to reduce pressure on the sails by easing the sheets. This is called 'spilling wind' and at the same time you maintain your course.

You will find this action is often required when sailing close-hauled or on a 'reach'. The same effect could be obtained by steering to bring the boat's head more towards the wind without easing the sheets; this is called 'luffing up'. It tends to slow your progress and it is up to you to choose which action to take to suit the conditions and situation at the time.

The advantage of 'spilling wind' is that you keep the boat upright and at the same time maintain your selected course.

HELMSMAN AND CREW, RESPONSIBILITIES

The helmsman and crew must, of course, work as a team. It is the responsibility of the helmsman to give clear and precise instructions to his crew as to what is to be done and it is the crew's responsibility to carry out those instructions exactly and promptly. All this talk of responsibilities sounds a bit ominous, but in fact when helmsman and crew have sailed together for a time you find that things are done almost automatically, the crew knows what to do in various situations and does it as a matter of course.

To illustrate the situation where the helmsman has to act let's refer to the action where we went through the steps of 'beating to windward'.

Assume that you are back in the boat in position 1, figure 9. You are on starboard tack and have cleared buoy A and decided that now is the time to 'go about'. Before altering course to bring the boat 'head to wind', position 2, you must warn the crew of your intentions. You do this by a loudly called warning of, "Ready about!" This warns the crew that you, the helmsman, intend to tack. The *immediate* response by the crew must be to ensure that the jib sheet is unjammed from the cleat and held by him (the crew) ready for the next move.

When you see that the crew has taken action to unjam the jib sheet, you then give the order, "Lee-ho!" which is a brief way of saying, "I am now putting the helm to the leeward." Having given this order you put the helm *down* to loo'ard and, as the boom swings across, you and the crew move over to the other side of the boat, taking care to balance the boat as he luffs up and heads through the eye of the wind to sale on the port tack.

During the above action there are two things which require careful timing, first by the crew to 'let fly' the port jib sheet, which must be done as the boat's head comes into the eye of the wind *and not before*, and as he moves across the boat he takes with him the starboard jib sheet which he hardens in as the boat takes up the port tack. The helmsman has to control the main sheet as he moves over on the new tack, at the same time controlling the tiller to maintain course. This will require moving the main sheet from his right hand to his left hand and the tiller from left hand to right hand. Both helmsman and crew will be sitting out on the weather side to balance the boat as the sails fill on the new tack. The above action is repeated each time you 'go about'!

In a dinghy, when sailing, the crew is regarded as being responsible for adjusting and handling the centre-board and everything forward of it, which includes the jib and the jib sheets, jib halyard, mainsail halyard, kicking strap, painter, paddles or oars, anchor, baler, jib stick, and last, but not least, keeping a look-out to warn the helmsman of obstructions.

The helmsman is responsible for handling the mainsail sheet, rudder and tiller, maintaining steerage way, keeping on course, making decisions and giving necessary orders for the efficient sailing of the boat and the safety of its occupants. When running before the wind the crew will move aft to balance the boat.

WEIGHT DISTRIBUTION

It is important on all points of sailing that the helmsman and crew place themselves correctly so as to balance the boat, to counter the heeling movement and keep the boat in as upright a position as possible bearing in mind the prevailing conditions of wind and weather.

When sailing close-hauled, and on a reach, both the helmsman and crew should be near midship and leaning out to counter the heeling movement of the boat due to the wind pressure on the sails.

When sailing on a run, and especially running 'goosewinged', both helmsman and crew should be towards the stern quarter one on each side to balance the boat and to prevent the bows 'digging in' due to the downward thrust on the bow caused by the pressure of the wind from astern.

COMING ALONGSIDE A JETTY AND PICKING UP A MOORING BUOY

To appreciate the various conditions which might exist in a manoeuvre to come alongside a jetty, or to pick up a mooring buoy, you should study the illustrations in figure 11. Here you will see four differing conditions, three for the jetty and one for a mooring buoy. We will refer to them as case A, B, C, and D.

In case A the wind and tide are both coming from

the same direction. The best approach to the jetty is shown, finishing head to wind and tide at the jetty. Make fast with the painter, lower the sails and raise the centre-board right up.

In case B the wind is blowing at right angles to the tide and directly towards the jetty so this makes things a little more complicated because of the wind blowing on to the jetty. You cannot go alongside the jetty broadside to the wind because the sails and mainsail boom would catch on the jetty and be damaged, so you have to head into the wind as shown, lower the mainsail, back the jib on the port side, and put the tiller over to starboard. The wind will push you back towards the jetty, and with the jib to port the bow will veer to starboard, the rudder will bring the stern to port and the *tide* will carry the boat back towards the jetty. You finish alongside head to tide, make fast and lower the jib, centre-board up.

In case C the wind is at right angles to the tide, but this time they are in the opposite direction from that shown in case B. However, the manoeuvre is not quite so complicated. Alternative methods of approach are shown. In the first (boat No. 1) the finish is *head to wind*, lowering the mainsail in the last few yards and relying on the boat's momentum to carry you to the jetty, the crew grabbing the jetty and making fast after letting the jib sheets fly. This requires careful judgement or you are liable to ram the jetty. Having made fast and lowered the jib the tide will push the boat round port side to the jetty, the boat lying head to tide, centre-board up.

In the alternative approach (boat No. 2) you come alongside *head to tide*. Let all the sheets fly as you run in, make fast, and lower the sails as quickly as possible, centre-board up. I have seen this manoeuvre used very successfully when a passenger was taken aboard at a jetty. The boat came alongside under similar conditions, but as they were only staying for a minute or two to pick up the extra passenger, the sails were not lowered, and centre-board left down, so after casting off they were able to get away again very quickly by hardening in the starboard jib sheet and, as the boat made way on wind and tide, the mainsail sheet was hardened in to set them on course on port tack.

In case D you are picking up a mooring buoy. Here the wind is directly opposite the run of the tide. The best approach is to beat to windward until near the buoy, then turn head to wind, lower the mainsail and turn to run up to the buoy under jib, letting the jib sheet fly as you near the buoy. The crew then makes fast to the buoy, lowers the jib and raises the centre-board. The boat is then lying head to tide.

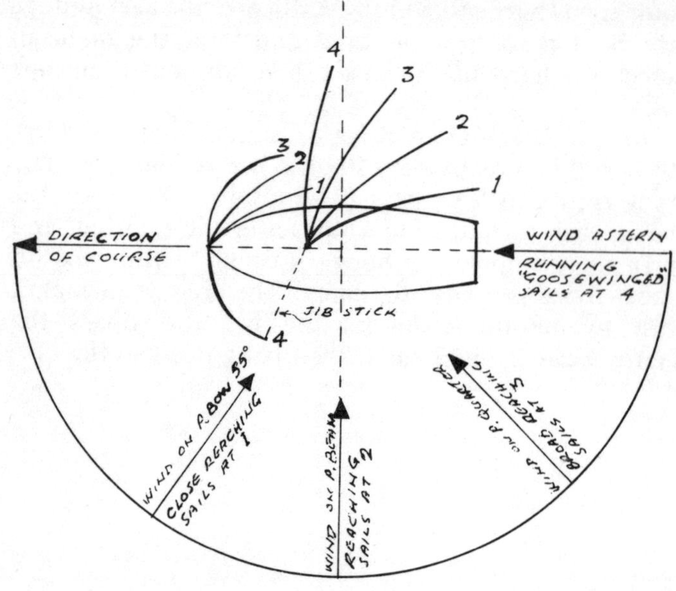

FIG 6
SAIL TRIMMING
FOR VARIOUS
WIND DIRECTIONS
IN RELATION TO SELECTED COURSE

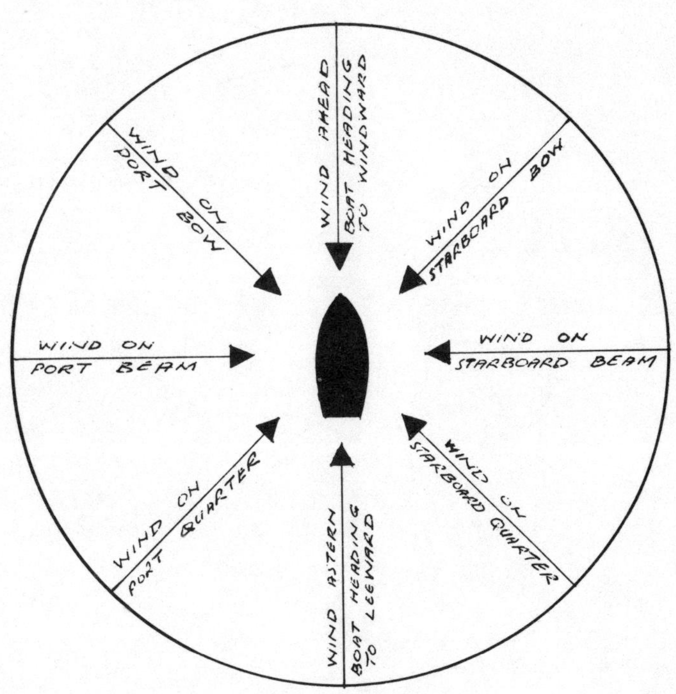

FIG. 7

WIND DIRECTION
IN RELATION TO BOAT'S HULL

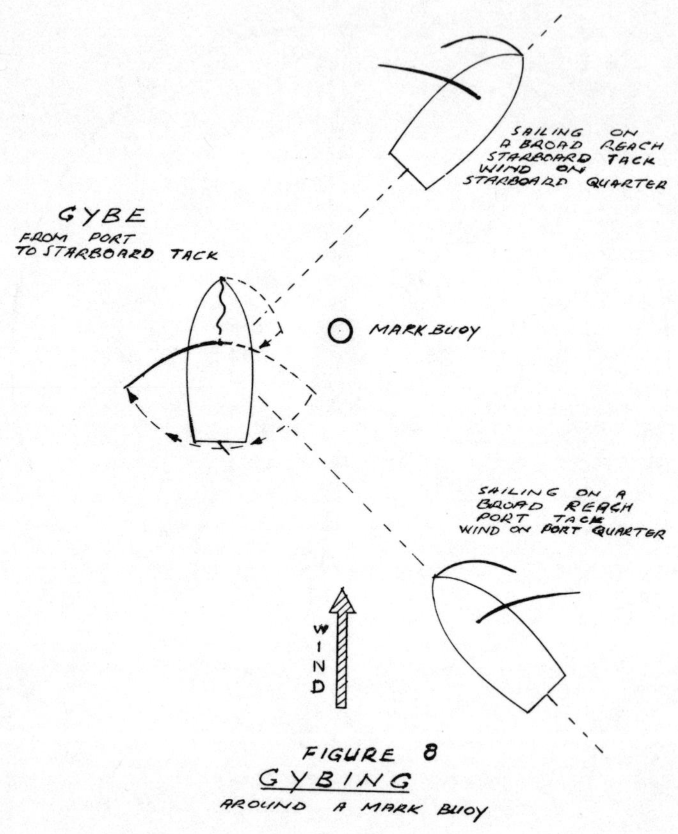

FIGURE 8
GYBING
AROUND A MARK BUOY

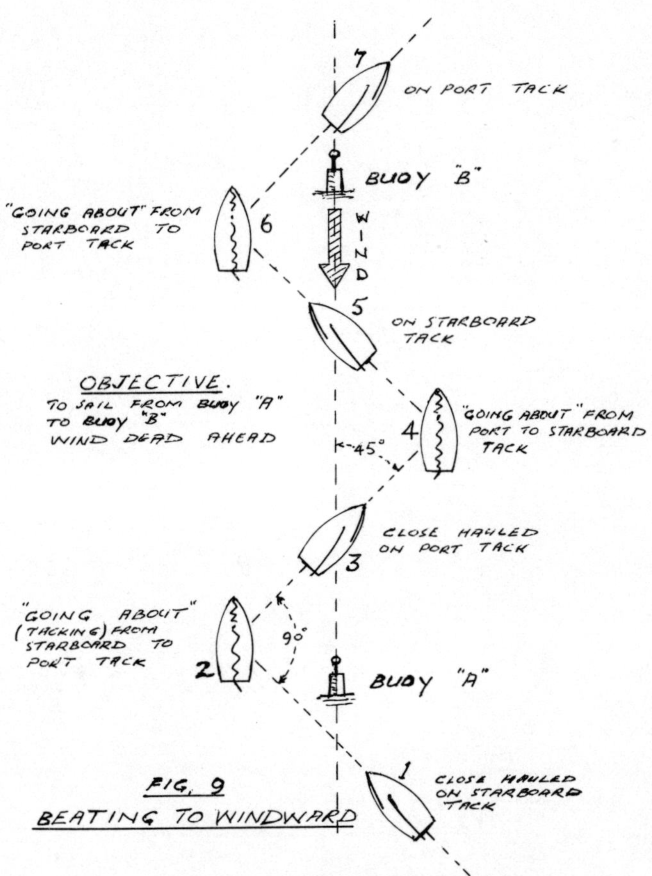

FIG. 9

BEATING TO WINDWARD

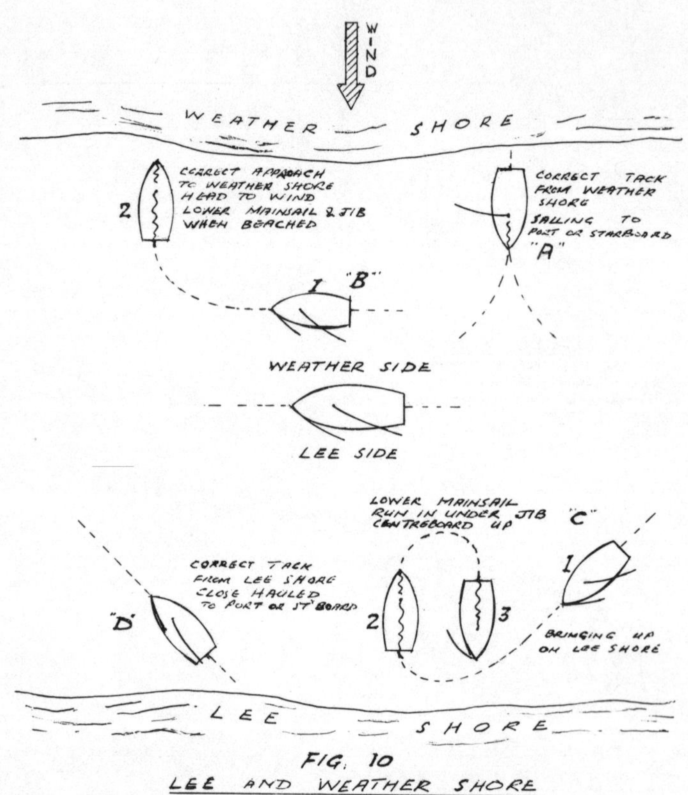

FIG. 10
LEE AND WEATHER SHORE

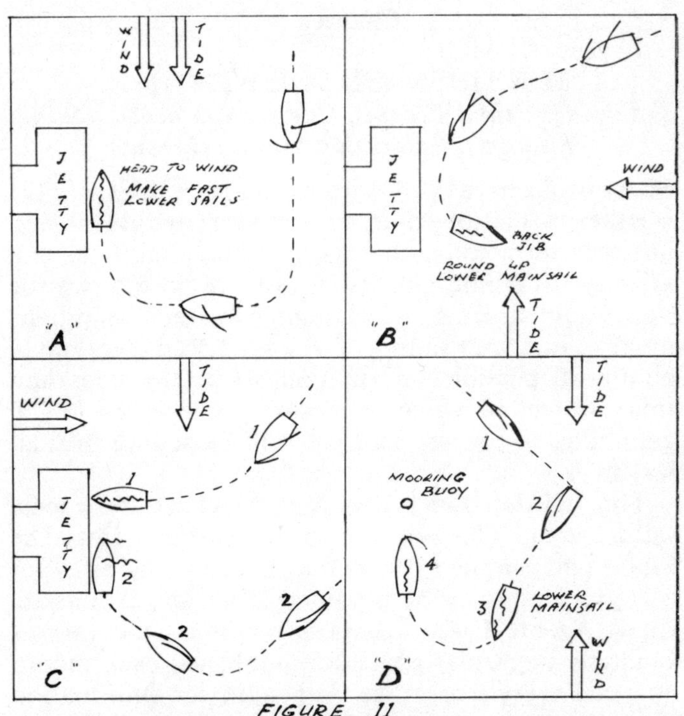

FIGURE 11
COMING ALONGSIDE A JETTY & PICKING UP
A MOORING BUOY
WITH VARIOUS TIDE AND WIND DIRECTIONS

Chapter 4

THE TIDES AND THE WEATHER
*Tidal water, tidal streams, tide tables (local), weather
forecasts, leeway due to cross currents*

Many books have been written about the tides and the
weather so it is not proposed to enlarge on this subject,
but only to mention that as the wind conditions can
affect your sailing and its enjoyment, so too can the
tides; tidal streams and changing weather conditions
make or mar your sailing. You are advised therefore to
obtain all possible information about the tides and
tidal streams in whatever locality you propose to sail
assuming, of course, that you will be sailing in tidal
waters.

The first step then is to purchase a chart of the local
sailing area. This you can usually obtain from the
local yacht chandler or you may have to send away for
a copy. They may be obtained from any Admiralty
Chart Agent. These agents advertise in the various
yachting magazines which are published each month
and one every week. See Appendix for information
regarding magazines and chart agents et cetera.

The chart will show soundings (depth of water) in
metres, areas which dry out at low water, main deep
water channels, or passages, which will be marked
with the appropriate channel buoys, red, or red and
white chequered for *port hand* marks and black and
black and white chequered conical buoys for

starboard hand marks. There may be other buoys marking middle ground or shallows and wrecks and these will be explained on the chart.

The channel buoys mark the edges of the navigable channels and they are set to indicate the channel edges when approaching the harbour from seawards.

You will be well advised to study the chart very carefully in every detail, for the more information you have regarding the area in which you sail, the more likely you are to be able to avoid situations that could be frustrating or even dangerous.

The chart will indicate areas that dry out at low water and tidal streams can be ascertained from the details on the chart. From this information you will know beforehand just where you can sail at *high water*, where you cannot sail at *low water*, and where to sail to avoid strong adverse tidal streams.

TIDE TABLES

The next step is to obtain a copy of the local tide tables. These may also be obtained from your local yacht chandler in the form of a small booklet for a few pence. The tide tables show the daily times and height of high and low water, neap tides and spring tides. The booklet will probably contain useful information on local tidal streams, all very helpful to the dinghy sailor.

WEATHER FORECASTS

Having decided to spend the day, or part of the day, in your sailing dinghy, always make a point of listening to the latest weather forecast on the radio before you set out from home. It is well known that the English weather conditions can change overnight, so don't risk it, check each morning and take heed of warnings of storm conditions or sea fog. The BBC radio 4 gives forecasts for inshore waters (up to 12 miles offshore). Details of precise times and frequencies are published in the *Radio Times*.

LEEWAY DUE TO TIDE AND CROSS CURRENTS

In chapter 3 it was pointed out that when sailing close-hauled, or on a reach, allowance must be made for leeway due to side thrust on the sails by the pressure of the wind.

You will probably be sailing in tidal waters so as well as having to make allowances for leeway due to the action of the wind, you are faced with the added problem of leeway due to the tide, tidal streams, and cross currents. All these can affect the dinghy's progress and, depending on the course of your dinghy relative to the movement of the water, the sideways drift will be decreased or increased. Let's take one or two examples. Suppose the wind and tide, or cross current, are moving in the same direction, then the leeway will be increased. If the tide is flowing against the wind the two forces could balance one another, result — no leeway. Again if you have a very strong tide flowing against a light wind, the leeway could be to windward instead of to leeward.

If the tide is flowing at right angles to the wind and you are sailing running before the wind, there would be a sideways drift with the tide. Again if you are sailing running before the wind and there is a following tide, i.e., wind and tide in the same direction, there would be no leeway.

In each case you have to judge the amount of leeway you are likely to make when sailing on any particular course, or trying to sail to a mark, and make allowances to counter it. You will, no doubt, realize by now that in many instances you cannot reach your destination or mark by sailing directly at it. In slack water you will have to steer for a point to windward of the mark and so allow for the effects of leeway, and in *tidal* waters allow for a plus or minus factor due to the effect of tide or tidal stream. Good judgement will only come with experience and a sound knowledge of local conditions, and so we come back to the fact that complete information about local tides, tidal streams and careful study of your local sailing area is of great importance if you are to obtain the best and most satisfactory results from your sailing activities.

Chapter 5

SAFETY IN A SAILING DINGHY AFLOAT
Equipment, anchors, warps, paddles, knots, swimming, clothing

Safety equipment in a sailing dinghy, when afloat, consists of two parts, that required for the safety of the boat and that required for the safety of the crew. In the case of the boat the equipment should consist of,

(a) *Buoyancy* — This will take the form of built-in water-tight tanks, or buoyancy bags filled with air and tied into position. The object of all this built-in or tied on buoyancy is to ensure that the dinghy will remain floating even if capsized and waterlogged and still be able to stay above water with the crew sitting on the upturned hull.

(b) A small anchor and Terylene anchor warp about 50ft long and about 1in. circumference.

(c) Two oars, or paddles.

(d) A plastic baler.

(e) A Terylene painter, about 30ft long and about 7/8in. circumference, to be used for making fast to a jetty or mooring, or for a tow et cetera. Could also be used to add to the anchor warp if required.

(f) For those who intend sailing any considerable distance out to sea some daylight distress signals are recommended as an added safety measure. These can be purchased from the local ship's chandler. These signals give off a cloud of bright orange smoke when opened, which can be seen for miles around. Sailing far out to sea in a small dinghy is not recommended, especially for beginners, however, there are always some who will venture too far.

Having carefully collected all the items required at some expense, you must take steps to make sure they are not lost overboard should you capsize, so all loose objects such as paddles, anchor, warps, baler et cetera, must be secured and lashed into the most convenient position in the boat so that they may be at hand when required.

Safety equipment for the crew consists of,
(a) Life-jackets (bright orange or yellow in colour). These may be purchased from the local ship's chandlers. They are made in many types, the best and most efficient being the one designed to keep the wearer's head out of the water. One well-known type is the 'Crewsaver' which has built-in buoyancy and may also be inflated for extra buoyancy. There are many other types of buoyancy aids on the market from which the dinghy sailor may choose.
(b) For night-time sailors (not recommended for beginners) a light attached to the life-jacket, in case of a fall overboard at night is necessary. This light is waterproof, battery operated and recommended for night sailing.
(c) A whistle attached to the life-jacket to attract attention, especially at night in case the light mentioned in (b) should fail, is recommended. Some life-jackets have whistles provided in a small pocket.
(d) A yacht knife with a sharp blade and a spike is very useful in many ways. This knife should be kept on a lanyard round the waist, with the knife in the pocket

of your shorts. One very good example of this type of yacht knife in stainless steel is the 'Currey Lockspike'. It is neat and flat and not too big. You should have your name engraved on the side.

(e) A bright orange or yellow waterproof smock is worn over the top of your clothing and will not only keep you dry in the boat but also, and this is the important point, is easily seen if you should fall overboard. These smocks are usually made of Bri-Nylon and they are very light in weight. Your local boat chandler will be able to supply all the items of equipment required for boat and crew.

CLOTHING

The question of what to wear when sailing is a matter of choice by each individual. The men and boys usually favour an old pair of shorts or jeans and a shirt, plus a pullover if the wind is chilly and topped off with the waterproof smock and trousers in the same waterproof material. The women and girls wear much the same sort of gear — nothing that would spoil if soaked in sea water and nothing showy. For the feet, wear yachting shoes, canvas with special grip rubber soles. On a hot summer's day one often sees the boys in shorts plus life-jacket and the girls in bikinis and life-jacket. What you wear depends a lot on the time of the year and the weather. The main thing is to keep dry and warm.

KNOTS

Some mention of various knots has been included in this chapter because it is important that you know what sort of knots to use under different conditions, how to tie up the dinghy to a bollard, a jetty, or to a mooring buoy so that it is safe and will not come loose and drift away, and in other circumstances when your own safety could depend on your ability to tie the right knot at the right time, quickly and without fumbling!

In figure 13 seven of the knots most used in connection with yachting are illustrated.

(1) *Figure of Eight*. This knot is used as a 'stopper' at the end of the jib sheets and the main sheet to prevent them from passing through the blocks or sheetleads.

(2) *Sheet Bend*. This knot is used for joining two ropes of unequal thickness.

(3) *Bowline*. When a loop is required that will not slip and tighten, the bowline is the knot used.

(4) *Reef knot*. A very easy knot to tie, useful for joining two ropes of the same thickness.

(5) *Fisherman's Bend*. A good secure knot for making a boat fast to a bollard or ring on a jetty or mooring buoy.

(6) *Round turn and two half hitches*. A good knot for making fast to a stanchion or mooring post. Easy to tie.

(7) *Clove Hitch*. A more simple type of knot for tying up to a mooring post or bollard. The main advantages of these nautical knots is that they are easy to tie and untie and they will not slip or come undone when in use. You are advised to practise these knots so that you can tie them in the dark if need be, and that could happen.

SWIMMING. SWIMMER OR NON-SWIMMER?

It is important that every member of the crew should be able to swim. The ability to swim has been included in this chapter as an additional safety factor regarding the crew. If you are a good swimmer it is an advantage and should give you a greater feeling of security when messing about in small boats.

It has often been said that people who cannot swim should not go out in small sailing dinghies, thus putting themselves, and those who might have to rescue them, at risk. To counter this it might be argued that with the use of modern efficient life-jackets the risk is minimized. However, there *is* a risk in certain circumstances and so, if you cannot swim and you wish to take up dinghy sailing, then go to the nearest swimming pool and have a qualified swimming instructor give you swimming lessons right away.

Chapter 6

EMERGENCY DRILL
Man overboard, capsize

MAN OVERBOARD

There may come a time when you will be faced with the problem of rescuing one of the crew who, by some misfortune, falls overboard. It is better to be prepared for this situation than to wait for it to happen and then find yourself wondering what to do.

The experts make certain recommendations but a lot depends on wind and tide conditions at the time. Don't be hasty and don't panic — remember the man in the water is wearing a life-jacket so he won't sink and you have time to size up the situation and decide on the best manoeuvre to avoid placing the boat and crew in jeopardy. Figure 12 shows two manoeuvres to effect a rescue.

In case A, *a fast gybe*, you are sailing close-hauled on port tack when one of the crew falls overboard (position 1). (What follows next is not recommended for sailing dinghies except in light winds for it could result in a capsize, then you're all in the water.) You put the tiller up to bear away to starboard and bring the boat to position 2 and gybe (position 3) and then on a beam reach on starboard tack (position 4). Luff up with the man slightly on the weather side (position 5) thus completing a rather tight circle. The rescued

54

person should be brought aboard *over the stern* and not over the side or you might capsize the boat.

You are advised to practise this manoeuvre under various wind conditions, throwing out a floating object to represent the man overboard, but start your practice runs in light winds.

Now consider case B, *bear away and tack back*, a manoeuvre favoured by many as being the safer for sailing dinghies in most wind conditions.

You are sailing close-hauled on starboard tack and one of the crew falls overboard (position 1). You put the tiller up and bear away on a beam reach, starboard tack (position 2) for a short distance and then go about on port tack (position 3). Bear away sharply on a broad reach still on port tack (position 4) to bring you nearer to the person in the water (position 5) and finally luff up with the man on the weather side (position 6). You are advised to practise this manoeuvre in various wind and tide conditions.

CAPSIZE

It is generally accepted that, sooner or later, the dinghy sailor will experience a capsize, caused maybe by a sudden gust of wind, or an involuntary gybe. Anyway, whatever the cause the boat is over and you and your crew are in the water and it's cold, so the sooner you get the boat righted and away the better.

Again don't panic, remember the boat won't sink, it has plenty of built-in buoyancy and you should be safe in your life-jacket. Now here is where your ability to swim could be very useful. For instance, if, when the boat heeled over, you were to be trapped under the mainsail, which by now is flat on the water, you, as a swimmer, should have no trouble getting out from under but a non-swimmer would probably panic and might need help.

So you're capsized, what to do? The first lesson is *stay with the boat* — hang on and don't let it get away from you. The next step is to right the boat. Under normal conditions this is usually an easy matter. The helmsman should màke his way to the centre-board, which will be sticking out from the hull in a horizontal position, and stand on it holding on to the gunwale and leaning back to lever the boat upright by using his own weight. At the same time the crew should have made his way to the bow to hold the boat head to wind. As the boat comes up the helmsman must hoist himself aboard and let free any sheets which may be jammed, usually the jib sheet, then bale out enough water so that she will sail, lower the sails if necessary, and then haul the crew inboard over the stern.

In theory it seems easy but only in practice will you find out what the difficulties might be. So once again you are advised to have a practice trial capsize, choosing your own conditions and a warm day if possible, and if you are not satisfied the first time, keep trying until you are satisfied that you have the drill more or less perfect.

Chapter 7

RULES OF THE ROAD
International regulations, prevention of collisions at sea

As with all other means of transport there are rules and regulations controlling the use and movement of boats and ships and these rules apply to sailing dinghies. Known as the 'International Regulations for the Prevention of Collisions at Sea' but generally referred to as the 'Rules of the Road', these regulations are published by Her Majesty's Stationery Office, London.

You need only concern yourself with the five basic rules which apply to sailing boats, which are,

1. When two boats under sail near each other are on the same tack the windward boat shall keep clear.

2. When two boats under sail are approaching each other on opposite tacks, the boat on port tack shall keep clear.

3. An overtaking boat shall keep clear of all boats, whether under power or sail, which it is overtaking.

4. A vessel driven by power shall keep clear of a vessel being driven only by sail except in a buoyed channel or a narrow channel which they cannot move out of. This means that if you, in your small dinghy, see a large ocean liner approaching you in a buoyed channel, *you must get out of its way* and be smart about it!

5. Sailing boats under power are regarded as power vessels for the purposes of these rules. This means that if you use an outboard engine to propel your dinghy you become a power boat. It should be noted that in most big and important harbours dealing with large ocean-going vessels there are local by-laws which give the large vessels the absolute right of way.

In dealing with the basic rules affecting the sail boats, you must, of course, realize that in some situations to insist on your rights could lead to a collision. Also, it is not good seamanship to put another boat into danger, so you give way in good time.

Apart from good seamanship and the right of way, there is the question of commonsense and courtesy. Remember too that the rules are intended for the safety of people operating small boats and large vessels.

I have seen cases of reckless and inconsiderate handling of boats and so far only by visiting motor boats and speedboats. The dictionary defines 'a reckless or inconsiderate motorist or cyclist' as a 'Road Hog'! I would define 'a reckless or inconsiderate and bad-mannered motorboatman, speedboatman or yachtsman', as a *Water Hog*!

So don't become a water hog and if you should be unfortunate enough to meet any then put them right and point out the error of their ways.

The following copy of a notice to mariners is considered relevant, and underlines the fact that there are obviously many boat users who are ignorant of the Rules of the Road, or such warnings from the local Harbour Master would not be necessary.

**Plymouth local notices to mariners No 11/74,
Dockyard Port of Plymouth**

1. No vessel (sail or power driven) shall, when navigating within the confined waters of the Port of Plymouth/Devonport hamper any other vessel which can navigate only within the narrow channels of the Dockyard Port.
2. The attention of all persons in charge of boats/ vessels is drawn to Rule 20 and 25c of the International Regulations for the Prevention of Collision at Sea.

Queen's Harbour Master,
Plymouth and Devonport,
28th February, 1974.

It should be noted that Harbour Masters have the power to take legal action against offenders who disregard the various regulations and fines up to £50 may be imposed. You have been cautioned.

Chapter 8

SIGNALS
The International Code of Signals, distress,
sound visual

This chapter has been included because most landlubbers are entirely ignorant of the meanings of the various signals flown, or sounded, by ships of all sizes and types, be they small workboats in a harbour or ocean-going vessels.

The 1969 edition of the International Code of Signals has been produced under the auspices of the Inter-governmental Maritime Consultative Organization, and published in England for the Department of Trade and Industry by Her Majesty's Stationery Office in London.

This code is used by vessels of most seafaring nations and you are advised to get to know those sections that, as a sailor, you should know.

The alphabetical flags, numeral pendants, substitutes, code and answering pendant are shown in figure 14, and the method of use is shown in the list of single letter signals as copied from the code.

Most of the International Code of Signals is only for the use of the larger yachts and ocean-going vessels, but there are some signals which could be used in a dinghy, and these would relate mainly to a situation of distress and emergency when you required help.

DISTRESS SIGNALS

These signals are to be used by a vessel in distress requiring assistance from other vessels or from the shore.

'10: a smoke signal giving off a volume of orange coloured smoke'.

'11: slowly and repeatedly raising and lowering arms outstretched to each side'.

N.B. 'The use of any of the foregoing signals, except for the purpose of indicating that a vessel is in distress, and the use of any signal which may be confused with any of the above signals is prohibited.'

In chapter five it was mentioned that daylight distress signals should be carried by those intending to sail out to sea, so that would comply with item 10 above.

SOUND SIGNALS

This refers to vessels of various sizes giving warning, on the siren, or foghorn, of a change of course.

One blast means, "I am changing course to starboard."

Two blasts means, "I am changing course to port."

Three blasts means, "Engines going astern."

If the vessel was stationary when she signalled three blasts then she will go astern. If under way at the time she signalled she will loose headway and may eventually go astern, maybe she is stopping to tie up to a buoy. Keep an eye on her, if you happen to be sailing near by.

VISUAL SIGNALS

About the only other signals with which you need concern yourself in your dinghy, are those hoisted ashore in the harbour. They relate to the weather, so watch out for them.

A black cone, point uppermost means a northerly gale is imminent.

A black cone, point downwards means a southerly gale is imminent.

Chapter 9

RIGGING THE BOAT
*Types of sails, the mast, the halyards,
standing rigging, running rigging, centre-board
and rudder*

The Mirror Class dinghy is gunter-rigged with the mainsail fixed to the gaff; the foresail, or jib, is triangular.

The word 'rigged' in this case is a sea-going term meaning equipped and ready to sail, and the name gunter-rig merely indicates that the mainsail is roughly triangular in shape and is fixed to a gaff, which in turn is attached to the mast and hoisted by means of a halyard (see figure 2 for details). It will be seen that the lower part of the luff of the mainsail (below the gaff) is laced to the mast.

It is essential to learn all the names of the various parts of the sails as shown in figure 2.

The term 'gunter-rig' is said to be derived from the days of Edmund Gunter (1581-1626) Professor of Astronomy at Gresham College, who invented, amongst other things, a sliding scale used in navigation. So, with the topmast, or gaff, and sail sliding up and down the lower mast on rings, it resembles Gunter's sliding scale. (The Mirror Dinghy uses lacing instead of rings.)

Now to the task of actually rigging the boat and preparing to launch it. It is assumed that the boat is new to you and therefore you are advised to choose a day with light breezes for your first try out. Carry out a trial run of rigging and hoisting sail before the actual launching in case any adjustments are found necessary.

Before starting to rig the boat place it bow to wind. Failure to do this could result in a capsize on the spot when you hoist the sails, and subsequent damage to the sails and rigging.

1. The first item to deal with is the mast and before stepping it in position you must secure the shrouds and forestay to the top of the mast and reeve the main halyard through the pulley at the mast top and also the jib halyard through its pulley near the mast top. Now step the mast by placing the base of the mast in the after mast stop and while you hold the mast, get someone to attach the shrouds to the shroud plates. After that the forestay must be made secure to the plate on the bow of the boat. See that the shrouds and forestay are tensioned sufficiently to support the mast at the correct angle.

It must be mentioned here that there are two types of rigging. Standing rigging, i.e., the shrouds and forestay supporting the mast, and running rigging consisting of the ropes, known as 'sheets', controlling the trim of the sails, i.e., mainsheet to the mainsail and jib sheets to the jib or foresail and also the halyards used to hoist the sails.

2. Put the sails' battens into the special pockets on the mainsail; the top batten is shorter than the others so take care to sort them out and get the right batten into the right pocket.

3. Secure the mainsail to the boom. In this case the sail is loose footed and is only secured at the clew and tack. Attach the tack first and then pull the foot of the sail taut and attach at the clew.

4. Secure the mainsail to the gaff by sliding the luff into the groove in the gaff and make fast at the head.
5. Fix the boom to the mast at the gooseneck fitting and attach the main halyard to the gaff. Reeve the main sheet through the main sheet pulley and leads fixed to the top of the transom and tie a figure of eight knot at the end of the sheet.
6. Fix the tack of the jib to the shackle at the stem head and then clip the luff hanks on to the forestay. Next fix the jib halyard to the head of the jib (by a shackle) and reeve the two jib sheets through the fairleads to port and starboard, not forgetting to put a figure of eight knot at the ends of each sheet so that they will not slip back through the fairleads.

Remember that the jib sheets must be led *inside* the shrouds or it will be impossible to adjust the jib properly when sailing.
7. The mainsail and jib are now ready for hoisting, but before doing so there are other items to see to.
8. Ship the rudder, i.e., fix the rudder on to its pintles on the transom and fix the lanyard so that the rudder blade is in the 'up' position.
9. Fix the tiller on to the head of the rudder stock.
10. Fix the burgee or racing flag halyard to the head of the gaff ready to hoist the burgee or racing flag before you launch the boat.

The burgee or racing flag acts as a wind indicator when sailing and it pays to keep an eye on it to obtain the best trim for the sails.

Sailing dinghies are not usually supplied with racing flags so you should visit the nearest boat chandler to obtain the necessary fitting. You can choose your own colour for the flag (see figure 2 for details of the burgee/racing flag).

The flag halyard is of light-weight cordage which runs through an eyelet near the top of the gaff and is made fast to a small cleat on the port side of the mast about 4ft above deck level.

If there is no eyelet on the gaff it is a simple matter to screw a small one, say ½in. at about 2in. from the top of the gaff on the port side. Use a chrome-plated or stainless steel eyelet to avoid rusting. Also fix a small cleat on the mast (port side) on which to secure the racing flag halyard.

11. Check that the centre-board retaining cord is in position.

12. Check that the oars or paddles are in the boat and secured and don't forget the baler.

13. Now having completed items 8, 9, 10, 11 and 12 get ready to hoist the mainsail first. Haul on the main halyard to hoist the gaff, having secured the lower end of the gaff to the mast as far as it will go up the mast, make fast (belay) to the cleat on the starboard side; make certain the fitting at the gooseneck, main boom to mast, is secure. Next lace the luff of the mainsail to the mast between the lower end of the gaff and the boom. Now attach and adjust the kicking strap to the boom. The purpose of the kicking strap is to stop the boom from lifting when sailing.

14. Now hoist the jib sail, by hauling on the jib halyard. Haul until the luff of the sail is taut otherwise the sail will not do its work properly. Secure (belay) the jib halyard to the cleat on the port side of the mast.

15. In securing the main and jib halyard to the cleats use two or three turns in a figure of eight and then form a loop, with the loose end to go over the cleat so that it does not get tangled up in the bottom of the boat.

At last you are ready to launch the boat and, if you and your crew have life-jackets on, get cracking, off you go.

ROUND THE MARKS, EXERCISE

Having dealt with all the points of sailing and various other matters covered by chapters 3 to 9 let us now go for a sail round the marks, an exercise that will give you the opportunity to put into practice some of the knowledge which you have gained.

Assume the course to be sailed as set out in figure 15 with the wind force 3, a gentle breeze, direction as shown blowing in line with mark 1 and the starting point and with mark 2 and mark 3.

The course consists of four legs of roughly a third to two-thirds of a mile each.

From the starting point, on a lee shore, to get to mark 1 you should start off close-hauled on starboard tack. This leg will take about three tacks to round the mark, you then trim sails on a close reach heading for mark 2, which could be done in one tack and allowing for leeway. To get round mark 2 you will have to gybe from port tack to starboard tack and then trim sails to run goosewinged before the wind. One tack will bring you to mark 3 and going about at this mark you should trim sails to run to the finishing point on a beam reach on starboard tack, again allowing for leeway, and as you near the shore, round up head to wind, lower mainsail and turn and run in under jib. Don't forget that centre-board as you get into shallow water, and the rudder!

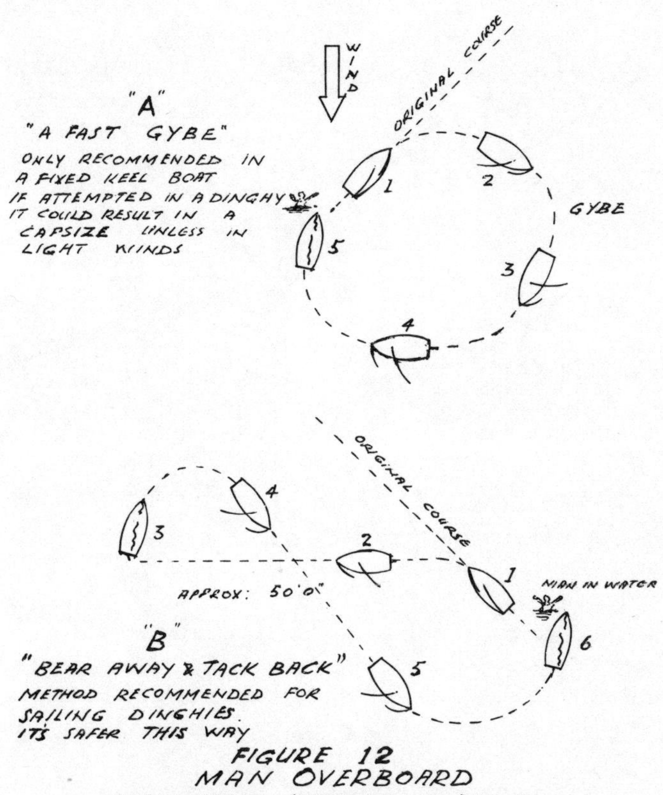

FIGURE 12
MAN OVERBOARD
ALTERNATIVE METHODS OF RESCUE

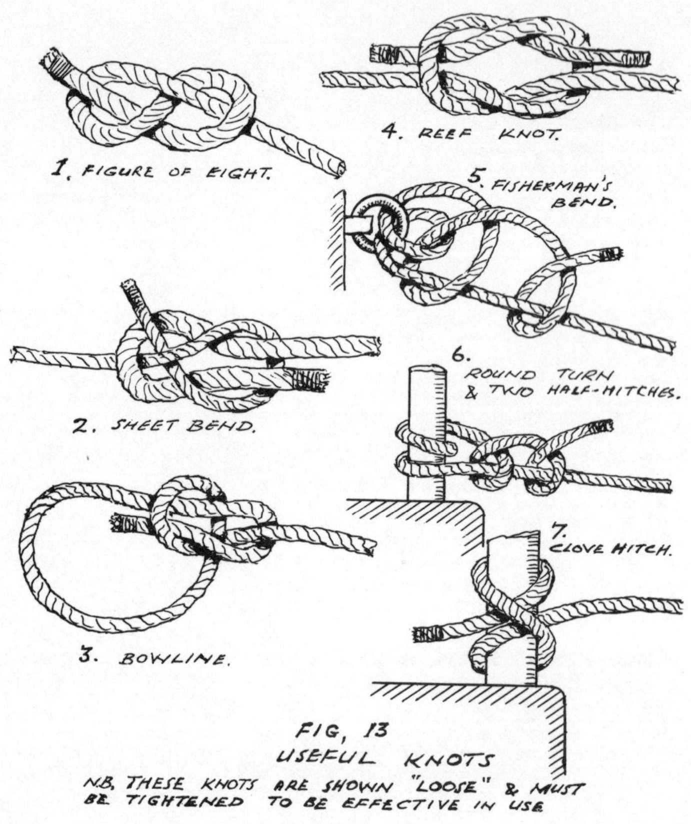

FIG. 13
USEFUL KNOTS
N.B. THESE KNOTS ARE SHOWN "LOOSE" & MUST BE TIGHTENED TO BE EFFECTIVE IN USE

THE INTERNATIONAL CODE OF SIGNALS
SINGLE LETTER SIGNALS

MAY BE MADE BY ANY METHOD OF SIGNALLING. FOR THOSE MARKED* SEE NOTE 1 BELOW.

A   I have a diver down; keep well clear at slow speed.

*B   I am taking in, or discharging, or carrying, dangerous goods.

C   Yes (affirmative or 'the significence of the previous group should be read in the affirmative').

*D   Keep clear of me; I am manoeuvring with difficulty.

*E   I am altering my course to starboard.

F   I am disabled; communicate with me.

G   I require a pilot. When made by fishing vessels operating in close proximity on the fishing grounds it means, "I am hauling nets."

*H   I have a pilot on board.

*I   I am altering my course to port.

J   I am on fire and have dangerous cargo on board; keep well clear of me.

*K   I wish to communicate with you.

L   You should stop your vessel instantly.

M   My vessel is stopped and making no way through the water.

N   No (negative or 'the significance of the previous group should be read in the negative'). This signal may be given only visually or by sound. For voice or radio transmission the signal should be 'NO'.

O   Man overboard.

P   In Harbour: All persons should report on board as the vessel is about to proceed to sea.
At sea: It may be used by fishing vessels to mean, "My nets have come fast upon an obstruction."

Q   My vessel is 'healthy' and I request free pratique.

*S   My engines are going astern.

*T   Keep clear of me; I am engaged in pair trawling.

U   You are running into danger.

V   I require assistance.

W   I require medical assistance.

X   Stop carrying out your intentions and watch for my signals.

Y   I am dragging my anchor.

Z   I require a tug. When made by fishing vessels operating in close proximity on the fishing grounds it means, "I am shooting nets."

NOTES:

1. Signals of letters marked * when made by sound may only be made in compliance with the requirements of the International Regulations for Preventing Collisions at Sea, Rules 15 and 28.

2. Signals K and S have special meanings as landing signals for small boats with crews or persons in distress (International Convention for the Safety of Life at Sea 1960 Chapter V Regulation 16).

INTERNATIONAL CODE OF SIGNALS
ALPHABETICAL FLAGS
A
B
C
D
E
F
G
H
I
J
K
L
M
N
O
P
Q
R
S
T
U
V
W
X
Y
Z
KEY TO COLOURS
WHITE
BLACK
RED
YELLOW
BLUE

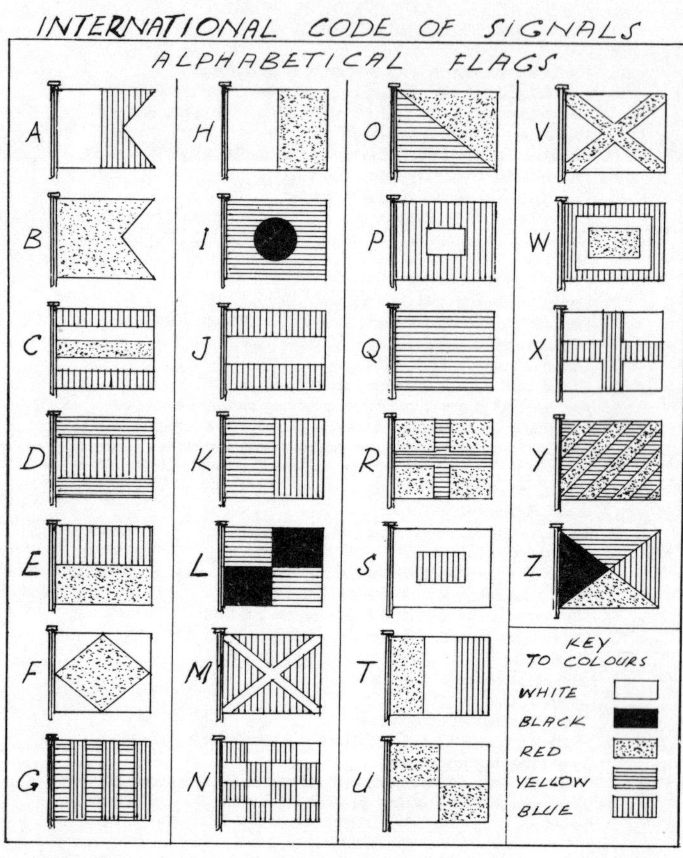

FIGURE 14

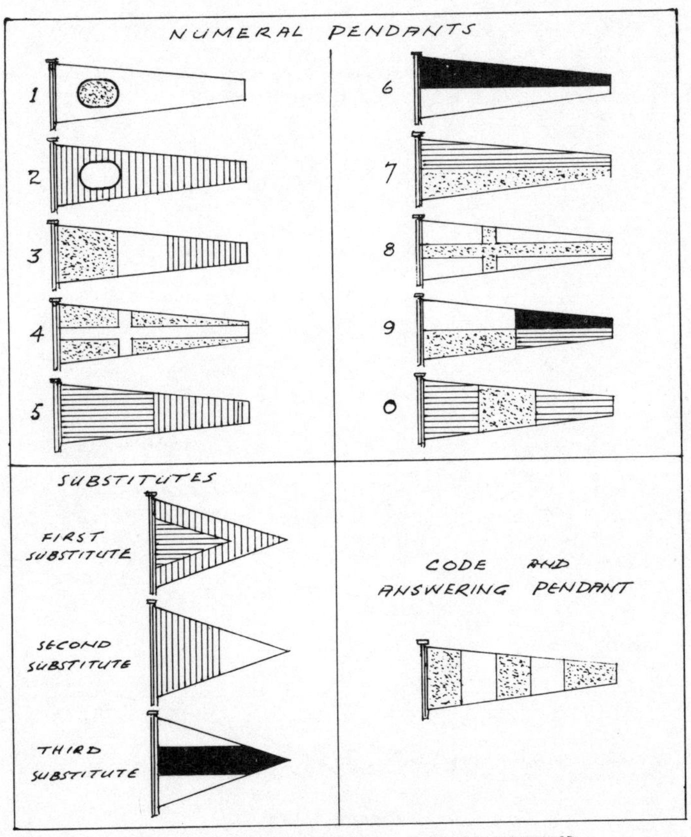

FIGURE 14 CONTINUED

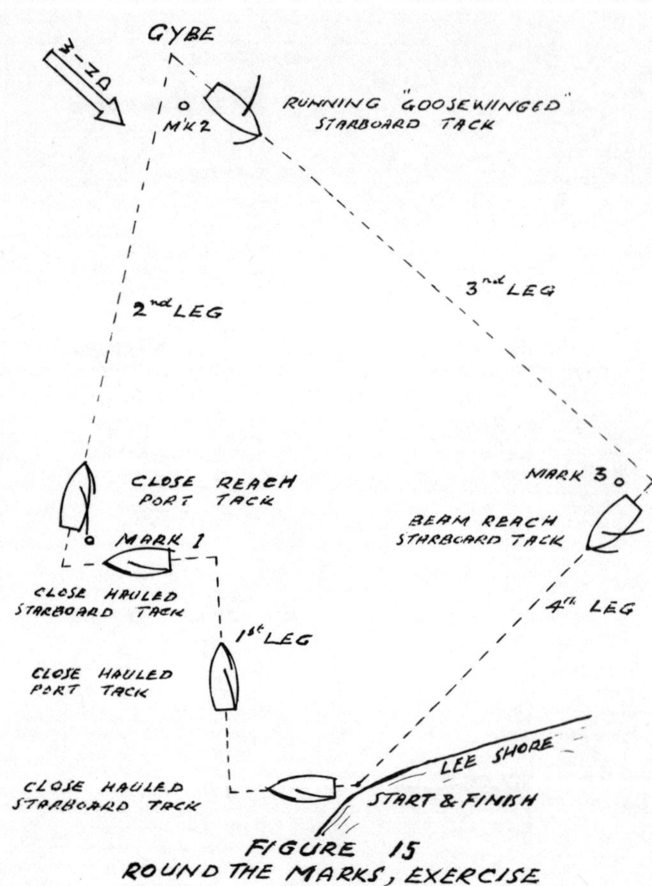

FIGURE 15
ROUND THE MARKS, EXERCISE

Chapter 10

Care and maintenance of the boat, winter storage, fitting out, insurance

This chapter could resolve itself into a list of do's and dont's. In the 'care and maintenance' of the boat, 'care' is meant to refer to the handling of the boat in such a manner as to avoid damage. By being 'careful' you will lessen the amount and cost of maintenance and repair work required at the end of each season.

For instance, when you run ashore, or beach the boat, don't leave it being bounced up and down by the waves on the deach, especially if the beach is pebbly. Also, instead of dragging the boat over the pebbles you, your crew, and a helper or two, could lift it over. This will save a great deal of wear on the hull.

When tied up to a jetty place fenders between the hull and the jetty to take the bumps and avoid damaging the hull.

Don't leave the sails flogging about in the wind when the boat is on the beach or at a mooring. A lot of damage can be done by such carelessness. The sails should be lowered and made secure, especially if the boat is to be there for any length of time.

Having finished your sailing for the day, the first thing is to lower and remove the sails, and remove the battens from their pockets. This will relieve the tension and help preserve the appearance of the sail.

Don't stow the battens in the sail bag with the sails, damage could result to both sails and battens. If the battens are made of wood, keep them in a dry place until required. Then the hull should be washed off, inside and outside, with fresh water to get rid of the salt (assuming you have been sailing on the sea). Most sailing clubs have a hose pipe available for this purpose, however a bucket of fresh water and a large sponge will do the job. It is good practice to dunk the sails in fresh water to get rid of the salt should they have had a ducking in the sea.

The boat should then be set up in its berth and the canvas boat cover should be secured so as to leave gaps for ventilation but keeping the rain out.

If the sails are wet take them home to be dried off out of doors over a clothes-line if possible, or spread them out on a dry lawn, if you are lucky enough to have a lawn. Never stow wet sails into a sailbag and forget about them for a week or more. If you do you will soon need new sails and they are expensive. Some jib sails usually have a wire rope in the luff so be careful when stowing this sail to *roll* it and not fold it. Start at the head and roll the wired luff in a coil, about a foot across, until the tack is reached.

If sails are to be stowed for long periods it is better not to put them in the sailbag but to hang them up in a dry place so that the air can circulate around them.

Maintenance of the boat during the season will consist of repairing any damage to the hull or paintwork. Deep scratches or bare wood should be dealt with right away and not left until next week or the week after. So have some filler and a pot of paint or varnish available.

Sails should be checked regularly for tears and

broken stitching and should be sent to the sailmaker for repairs.

Sheets, halyards and shrouds, forestay and kicking strap should be checked each time before setting sail.

Shrouds and forestay should be replaced if there is any sign of damage. Don't risk it, a broken shroud or stay when sailing could result in a broken mast and they *are* expensive, a new shroud or stay costs only a few pence.

Check the rudder and centre-board regularly and make sure that they are in good working order. Replace the lanyard to the rudder if it shows signs of wear.

Check the mast and gaff and main boom for wear and touch up with varnish any bare patches.

Unstep the mast from time to time and check the base of the mast and also the mast socket, where the water will lie and could cause rot; dry out the socket and apply several coats of marine varnish.

Special arrangements are usually required for winter storage of the boat and all the fittings.

The first thing is to find somewhere to keep the boat under cover and in a dry place. Most yacht clubs have no covered winter storage accommodation and so you must arrange for winter storage with a boatyard if you have no place at home for the boat. You are advised to book early with your local boatyard, well before the end of the season, or you may be disappointed.

Now to prepare the boat and fittings for the long winter lay-up.

The first task is to get rid of the salt from the hull, sails and rigging. This entails a thorough washing with fresh water, and then drying off. Having removed the battens the sails should be carefully washed and as those on a Mirror dinghy are fairly small they can usually be dunked in fresh cold water in the bath and then put out in the open air to dry.

The wire rope shrouds and forestay should be smeared with a light grease and stored away from items which might be damaged if in contact with grease. All metal fittings remaining on the boat should be smeared with grease during the storage period.

The mast, gaff, mainboom should be washed in fresh water and when dry should be touched up with varnish on any bare or rubbed patches. If you are storing these items, they should be slung up in a dry place and given plenty of support so they will not sag.

All sheets, halyards, warps and lacings should also be washed in fresh water and dried off before storing.

Remove from the boat all items such as paddles, rudder, tiller, centre-board and wash off with fresh water. When dry touch up bare patches with marine varnish, or paint, whichever is required.

Sails, halyards and sheets should be stored in a dry place where the air can circulate around them. If there is any damage to the sails send them to the sailmaker for repairs, so that they will be ready for the start of the next season. If you are fortunate enough to have a suitable place in which to store the hull, then place it up on trestles and make sure that it is well supported in several places to spread the weight. Examine the hull for damage and bare patches and treat accordingly. Do not leave this sort of work until the next season or the damp could get into the plywood and cause more damage.

With regard to fitting out for the next season, some owners prefer to leave everything until the springtime and then do a rather hurried job of preparing the boat, while others like to spread the work over the late autumn and early spring, thus taking more time over the work and, of course, doing a better job. The major work is the preparation of the hull, which usually requires rubbing down with wet and dry sand-paper and revarnishing, using a good quality marine varnish from your local boat chandler. This work could well be done in the autumn before the cold damp winter weather sets in, leaving the easier jobs to be tackled in the early spring. You will then have your dinghy ready in good time for the start of the new sailing season.

The question of insurance must not be overlooked. Your dinghy, with all its fittings and sails, represents a valuable investment and insurance against damage or loss is a must. Your local insurance agent can arrange marine insurance for you. The policy should also include cover for the crew. The premium is small, about £3.00 for a Mirror dinghy.

Chapter 11

Other types of dinghies. Family dinghies, racing dinghies

It may not generally be known that there are hundreds of different types of sailing dinghies in use all over the world and a large number of these craft are in the British Isles. The Sailing Dinghies Boat World Guide No 1, 1974 Edition lists 240 various types in use in the United Kingdom. It is not proposed to list all these different types but to mention some of the most modern types which have become very popular.

The following class dinghies may be divided into what may be regarded as 'family dinghies' and 'racing dinghies'.

Class	Length x beam	Type
The Wayfarer	15'10" x 6'1"	Family Dinghy
The Hornet	16'0" x 4'7"	Racing -
G.P. 14	14'0" x 5'0"	Family -
The Osprey	17'7" x 5'9"	Racing -
The Scorpion	14'0" x 4'10"	Racing -
Flying 15	20'0" x 5'0"	Racing -
Flying Dutchman	19'10½" x 5'7"	Racing -
International 470	15'5" x 5'7"	Racing -

It is considered that these eight classes of dinghies would give anyone wishing to progress from the small Mirror Class dinghy an interesting choice between the purely family boat and the faster racing craft according to one's family interests and family bank balance for, unfortunately, the cost of sailing dinghies is going up like everything else that requires highly skilled craftsmen to produce them.

Most of these classes of boats can now be obtained in glass reinforced plastic, G.R.P. for short, which most dinghy enthusiasts seem to prefer as it lessens the amount of maintenance work required on the hull.

Chapter 12

Joining a sailing club and the Royal Yachting Association, books, magazines, the frostbiters

No doubt most newcomers to dinghy sailing have difficulty in deciding whether it is worth joining a sailing club and, of course, they are not in a position to be aware of the many advantages arising from membership of even the smallest of clubs.

You have now acquired your sailing dinghy, so where are you going to berth it and sail it in the summer? If you live in a seaside town there are certain to be several yacht clubs and sailing clubs in operation. Make your choice and apply for membership, but first find out which club has a fleet of your class of dinghy so that if you become a member you can eventually join in the various events, including racing, organized for that class. Most experienced dinghy sailors will tell you that once you have learnt to handle your dinghy and to sail her reasonably well, the sooner you start racing the better, for once you start racing, your lack of experience as a helmsman will show and you will learn quickly by observing what the experts do and discussing tactics with them.

If you live inland you will have to decide on whether to sail on inland waters or to take the boat to a seaside town or port. Having decided on the most suitable, or most convenient, inland waters, port or town, you will need a place to berth the boat for the season and so you will be well advised to join a sailing club as soon as possible and apply for a berth. Most clubs cater for cadet members between the ages of twelve and eighteen at a reduced subscription.

The advantages of club membership are many, and may be summarized as follows. You have the use of a berth for the boat and usually a slipway for launching; clubhouse, lounge, yachting periodicals, bar (soft drinks only for those under eighteen), changing rooms, washing, shower, toilets, teas and snacks. Some clubs provide lockers for storing sailing gear; facilities for washing off the boat, organized sailing events and racing, and last, but not least, meeting experienced dinghy sailors and yachtsmen, from whom you can gain useful advice and information. You will only have the benefit of all these things in an established sailing club.

The Royal Yachting Association is the governing body for all matters relating to yachting and dinghy sailing, and international racing is under the control of the International Yacht Racing Union.

Racing rules have been laid down by the R.Y.A. so, when you become experienced enough to race, you will need to study these rules before you compete in any races. You would be well advised to become a member of the R.Y.A. to obtain some of the many useful books and pamphlets which they publish from time to time. There is also an advice service on sailing matters which is free to members.

More clubs are organizing winter sailing and racing because an increasing number of dinghy owners are not satisfied that they are getting enough out of owning a boat which normally is used only for a short period each year. These hardy types wear special sailing gear, i.e., wet suits et cetera, and have come to be known as the 'Frostbiters'.

There are many more advanced and technical books available, should the reader wish to extend his knowledge on the technical side, such as coastal navigation for those who may wish to acquire a larger boat in the future in order to try their hand at cruising with the family.

There are several well illustrated yachting magazines published each month and one published weekly. These magazines are a useful source of information on yachts and dinghies, fittings, sailing gear et cetera, and keep one up-to-date with the latest news of the yachting and boating world. The weekly magazine deals mainly with dinghy sailing.

APPENDIX

Books

Coastwise Navigation (Reprinted 1972) G.G. Watkins
Kandy Publications

*Sailing Dinghies Boat World Guide No. 1 1974
Edition* Boat World Sells Publications Ltd.

*Yacht Racing: including the International Racing
rules* YPI/69 Royal Yachting Association, Victoria
Way, Woking, Surrey GU21 1EQ

Magazines

Yachting World	IPC Transport Press Ltd.
Yachting, Monthly	IPC Magazines Ltd.
Yachting and Boating weekly	Haymarket Publishing Ltd.
Dinghy Sailing	Prenbourne Publishing Ltd.

Addresses

The Royal Yachting Association	Victoria Way, Woking, Surrey GU21 1EQ.
Meteorological Office	See Local Telephone Directory
Coastguard Station	See Local Telephone Directory

84

Port & Coastal Charts	H.M. Stationery Office, Atlantic House, Holborn Viaduct, London EC1P 1BN.
Port & Coastal Charts	Can usually be obtained in your local port from ships' chandlers.
Port & Coastal Charts	Captain O.M. Watts Ltd. 45 Albermarle Street, Piccadilly, London, W.1.
Stanford's Charts	Stanford Maritime Ltd. 12-14 Long Acre, London WC2E 9LP

INDEX

Fairleads, 64
Figure of eight knot, 51, 64, 68
Fisherman's bend, 51, 68
Flag, racing, 64
Fitting out, 76-77
Flying Dutchman, 78
'Flying 15', 78
Fog, warnings, 46
Foot, of sail, 27, 63
Foresail, 19
Forestay, 63, 64, 75
Frostbiters, the, 82

Gaff, 62, 64, 65, 75
Going about, 26, 33
Gooseneck, 64, 65
'GP 14', 78
Gunter rig, 62
Gunwale, 55
Gybing, 29-30, 40, 53

Halyards, 34, 63, 64, 65
Hanks, luff, 64
Harbour Masters, 57, 58
Head, of sail, 19
Helmsman, 27, 33-35, 55
Hornet, the, 78
Hull, 18, 73, 74, 75, 76, 77

In irons, 30
Insurance, marine, 77
"International 470", 78
International Regulations, 56-57

Jamming Cleat, 27
Jetty, 35-37
Jib, 17, 19, 63, 64, 65
Jib Sheet, 27
Jib Stick, 28

Kicking strap, 34, 65
Knife, yacht, 49-50
Knots, 50-51, 68

Lacing, luff to mast, 62, 65
Lanyard, rudder, 64